THE OFFICIAL
ANNUAL
2012

Written by Douglas Russell
Designed by Colin Heggie

A Grange Publication

© 2011. Published by Grange Communications Ltd., Edinburgh, under licence from Rangers Football Club. Printed in the EU.

Photographs © Rangers Football Club, Kirk O'Rourke & Aileen Wilson

ISBN 978 1 908221 33 9

£7.99

CONTENTS

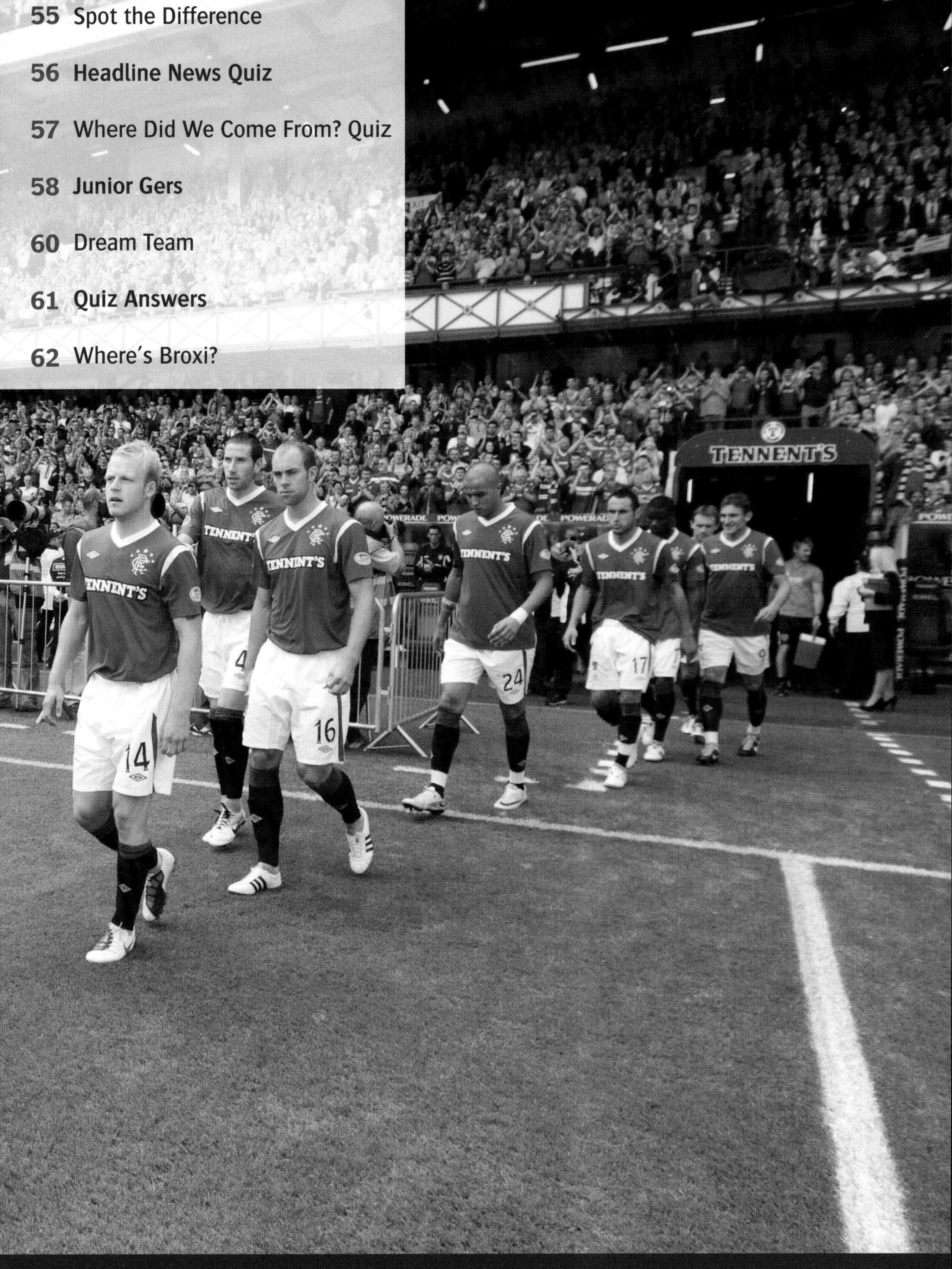

TENNENT'S

THE 2010/11 SPL CAMPAIGN

Three in a row champions!

AUGUST

The opening day's quickest SPL goal was scored by Kenny Miller against **Kilmarnock** after a goal line clearance from Kirk Broadfoot's rasping shot rebounded off his back and into the net. Early in the second period, Rangers doubled their advantage with a delightful goal when Steven Naismith drilled home inside the far post after an intelligent, lofted pass on the break from Miller. The visitors pulled one back from the penalty spot almost immediately but the Light Blues held firm at 2-1 to secure three points.

Away to **Hibernian** at Easter Road, Kenny Miller was at his most lethal and hit all three second half Rangers goals in a comprehensive 3-0 win. This was the striker's first hat-trick for the Club since netting five against St Mirren in Season 2000/01. His first and second of the afternoon were right foot finishes past Mark Brown after passes from James Beattie and Vladimir Weiss respectively. Then, following a Steven Davis ball from wide left that split the home defence, he thundered a left foot drive across the keeper into the far corner to complete the scoring and another capital performance by the league champions.

St Johnstone made an ideal start at Ibrox with a goal midway through the first period. However Sasa Papac, with his third goal in two seasons against the team from Perth, levelled for Rangers almost immediately after the keeper could only parry a powerful Steven Naismith header from close range. In the second half, Lee McCulloch passed into space ahead of Kenny Miller who out-muscled defender Maybury before hitting a glorious

shot with the outside of his boot. After the ball arced past Graeme Smith into the net, fans rose to acclaim both the winner and goal number 50 of his Rangers career.

SEPTEMBER

Walter Smith's side then recorded their third 2-1 victory in four league games. With less than ten minutes played at New Douglas Park against **Hamilton Academical**, Nikica Jelvic scored his first goal for the Club with a clinical header following clever play down the left by Kyle Lafferty and his subsequent cross into the danger zone. A Madjid Bougherra own goal shortly after the break cancelled Rangers advantage but substitute Kenny Miller was once again the headline maker when he made sure of the points right at the end of the game. On this occasion, the striker's perfect chip from Lee McCulloch's through ball beat Czech keeper Cerny for his sixth goal in four SPL fixtures.

Four days after securing a point against Manchester United at Old Trafford in the UEFA Champions League, Rangers turned on the style against **Dundee United** at Ibrox. Although Sean Dillon's own goal (from a Steven Davis low drive across the box) was all that separated the teams at the break, second half goals from Kenny Miller (2) and substitute Steven Naismith confirmed an impressive 4-0 win. Miller's strike partner Nikica Jelavic teed up the Scot for both of his goals whilst David Weir's lofted ball into the penalty area was the key to Naismith's headed finish. Man-of-the-match, however, was winger Vladimir Weiss who enthralled the Ibrox crowd with a delightful display of trickery and skill.

Despite being two goals down after thirty minutes, Rangers fought back to record a memorable 3-2 away win against **Aberdeen**. Kenny Miller netted from the penalty spot (after Vladimir Weiss had been felled in the box) just before the break to give his side a valuable lifeline. Then, in the second half, Miller scored again when he swept high into the net after a move involving both Steven Naismith and Steven Davis. The winner was courtesy of Nikica Jelavic who stroked home with an assured finish after Naismith, beating the offside trap, ran from the halfway mark before drawing the keeper and setting-up the Croatian international. This was Rangers first win at Pittodrie since December 2006.

OCTOBER

At Tynecastle, **Hearts** led for most of the game thanks to a goal early in the first half. Although Sasa Papac smacked the base of the post in the second period, the away fans had to wait until ten minutes before the end to celebrate when substitute Kyle Lafferty's low free kick evaded the defensive wall to find the bottom corner of the net. In a dramatic finish, Steven Davis also struck woodwork before the Light Blues secured another important victory right at the end of the game. Steven Naismith – completing an excellent seven days for the Club following his display at Pittodrie the previous Sunday and his winning goal in the midweek UEFA Champions League victory over Turkish champions Bursapor - ran from deep before exchanging passes with Lafferty and firing home with the outside of his right boot.

Craig Brown's **Motherwell** arrived at Ibrox in fine form having won all their away fixtures since the start of the SPL campaign and, for the third successive SPL encounter, Rangers trailed at the interval. However, Steven Naismith equalised at the start of the second period before midfielder Steven Davis made it 2-1 with a super solo effort after cutting through the centre of the visitors' rearguard to fire home from 18 yards. Additional goals by Kenny Miller (from Naismith's clever cross) and Vladimir Weiss – his first for the Club – secured an emphatic 4-1 triumph against the side that before this game had not conceded a single goal away from Fir Park in any 2010/11 league fixture.

On derby day in the east end of Glasgow, Kenny Miller netted a double for the third match in a row in the opening Old Firm clash of an SPL campaign. Although Hooper scored for **Celtic** on the stroke of half time, Rangers drew level very early in the second period when Kyle Lafferty met a Steven Davis delivery into the box and the ball hit off Loovens before nestling in the back of the net. Miller, with a sensational right foot volley, doubled his side's tally when he rifled home a loose ball following a block on Maurice Edu. Then, after Kirk Broadfoot was fouled in the area, Miller made it 3-1 from the penalty spot for his 13th goal in nine SPL games.

Maurice Edu, following a precise pass from midfield partner Steven Davis, scored early-on against **Inverness Caley Thistle** at Ibrox with a fine left foot strike. However, a late equaliser meant that Terry Butcher's men denied the Light Blues a 10th consecutive league win for the first time in over a century. The last time the Club achieved this unique feat was back in 1898 when Rangers remained unbeaten in the league for the entire season.

NOVEMBER

After a first half without goals in Paisley, a chipped ball into the box from Steven Davis at the beginning of the second period caused the confusion that led to a **St Mirren** own goal. Steven Naismith, with his eighth of the season, doubled the Champions' tally following a tap-in from close range after good play down the left wing by substitute Kyle Lafferty. Kenny Miller then made it three when he confidently converted a Lee McCulloch long ball down the middle before the home side claimed a consolation goal from the penalty spot.

An unbeaten 34 match sequence of domestic league and cup games at Ibrox came to an end with **Hibernian's** 3-0 SPL win. This was Colin Calderwood's first win since his appointment as manager of the Edinburgh team. To compound matters for Rangers, Maurice Edu and Sasa Papac were both injured and stretchered off within minutes of each other shortly before the break.

First half strikes from Kenny Miller and Vladimir Weiss made certain of a home win against **Aberdeen** the next week. Scotland striker Miller opened the scoring with a perfectly judged head flick from an inviting Weiss cross before the Slovak footballer himself crashed home past Langfield with a powerful drive for his second goal of the league campaign. Although the Light Blues could have increased their tally - Miller missed a penalty just before the break - the score remained 2-0.

Rangers then faced a **Kilmarnock** side that had won three of their last four league games by a 3-0 margin. Local hero Conor Sammon netted midway through the first period at Rugby Park but Kenny Miller equalised from the penalty spot just before the interval after he was felled in the box. Shortly after the break, Miller scored with another penalty kick following a foul on Kyle Lafferty before Sammon claimed his second of the afternoon. Then, after Steven Whittaker's pin-point cross into the box, Kenny Miller blasted home from close range for the winner, his hat-trick and another three crucial points in the league race. This was the sixth time in 14 games that Rangers had achieved victory after going a goal behind.

DECEMBER

At **Inverness Caley Thistle**, the only goal of the first period was a magnificent long-range strike by Jonny Hayes that gave the Highland outfit a deserved lead. Kenny Miller, with a clinical right foot drive, made it 1-1 early in the second half as Rangers began to dominate. However, despite opportunities to win the game – Miller missed a penalty for example – Walter Smith's men had to settle for a draw, dropping points away from home for the first time this season.

Ending 2010 in fine form however, Rangers turned on the style against **Motherwell** to record their first Fir Park win in three years. Kenny Miller claimed the opener when he slotted home following Madjid Bougherra's low cross from the right. A Saunders own goal (from a Vladimir Weiss free-kick into the penalty area) then doubled the visitors' advantage before the break. Motherwell hit back to score at the start of the second half but additional goals from Weiss (a super solo effort) and Miller (from another clever Weiss free-kick into the box) confirmed an impressive 4-1 win at a difficult venue.

JANUARY

Prior to the second Old Firm clash of the campaign on the 40th Anniversary of the Ibrox Disaster, former captains John Greig and Billy McNeill joined players and officials to observe a minute's silence for the 66 fans who died on Stairway 13 on 2 January 1971. With an air of sadness hanging over the stadium, Rangers started the game with real purpose and Lee McCulloch came close when his net bound header was nudged on to the bar by full back Izaguirre. **Celtic**, however, eventually won 2-0 after a second half brace from Greek striker Samaras.

Vladimir Weiss lit up Ibrox on a dull winter's afternoon with a superlative display against **Hamilton Academical** and scored twice in a 4-0 victory. The winger's first goal was a right foot drive from 25 yards that flew low past the keeper. Then, after winning a penalty which Steven Whittaker duly converted, the Slovak claimed his second of the game when he found the bottom corner with a curling free-kick on the stroke of half time. Late in the second period, substitute Maurice Edu completed the quartet of goals with a crisp left foot shot from the edge of the area following Whittaker's throw-in.

Both previous 2010/11 meetings with **Inverness Caley Thistle** ended in 1-1 draws. At Ibrox, there was little between the teams once again but this time Rangers secured all three points after Steven Davis scored the only goal of the game on the stroke of half time. His

right foot strike from just outside the penalty area - after being set-up by Lee McCulloch - was low, firm and true, beating keeper Esson to find the bottom corner of the net.

Walter Smith's side created numerous chances and dominated the first half of a pulsating Tynecastle clash but **Hearts** keeper Marian Kello was in international form with a string of superb saves. Late in the second period, the home side edged ahead when Rangers lost a scrappy goal before substitute Nikica Jelavic came close to salvaging a point with a thunderous drive that crashed off the underside of the crossbar. This 1-0 reversal was Rangers first away defeat of the league campaign.

Back in Edinburgh for the second time in four days, Rangers returned to winning ways and defeated **Hibernian** 2-0 at Easter Road. Both goals were scored in the first half. Defender Madjid Bougherra, with his first of the season, netted with a low drive from the corner of the box following a Vladimir Weiss free-kick. Nikica Jelavic then doubled Rangers advantage when he intercepted a back-pass and rounded keeper Smith before stroking home from a tight angle.

FEBRUARY

Shortly after kick-off against **Hearts** at Ibrox, Kyle Lafferty scored the only goal of the game when he volleyed home from fifteen yards following Steven Whittaker's perfectly judged diagonal ball into the penalty area. New signing El Hadji Diouf from Blackburn Rovers impressed after coming on as a first half substitute for the injured Lee McCulloch and, right at the end, keeper Kello could only parry a powerful drive by the former African Player of the Year but Steven Davis was ruled offside netting the rebound.

Nikica Jelavic claimed the first hat-trick of his Rangers career against **Motherwell** as the Light Blues recorded their biggest win of the season with a 6-0 rout. Shortly after kick-off, Steven Naismith was first on the score sheet when he slid home a Vladimir Weiss delivery from the left. Jelavic then netted twice before half time with right foot finishes after Steven Whittaker and Weiss respectively had supplied the Croatian striker with opportunities. In the second period, following a Hutchison own goal, Jelavic completed his treble with a volley that squirmed away from the keeper. One of the biggest cheers of the day however was reserved for substitute David Healy when the lifelong Rangers fan netted from close range near the end.

Walter Smith's side subsequently lost ground in the league campaign after **Celtic's** emphatic 3-0 win in the third Old Firm league encounter of the season at Celtic Park.

Three days on from the Europa League triumph against Sporting Lisbon in Portugal, Rangers defeated **St Johnstone** 4-0 at Ibrox. Nikica Jelavic claimed an early opener with a powerful left foot drive before Kyle Lafferty doubled the advantage when he headed past Enckelman from a Gregg Wylde corner just before the interval. Late in the second period, Sasa Papac scored his fourth goal against St Johnstone in two seasons after he slotted beyond the keeper following Jelavic's delightful back heel pass. Then, right at the end, the Croatian forward slammed a loose ball into the corner of the net to complete his double and a fine all-round display by the team.

MARCH

Against **St Mirren** in Paisley, Kyle Bartley scored the only goal of the game midway through the first half when he headed home from an inviting Madjid Bougherra cross into the box. It was the youngster's first goal for the Club since arriving on-loan from Arsenal in the January transfer window.

Rangers then faced fourth-placed **Kilmarnock** at home. El-Hadji Diouf opened the scoring shortly before the break after blasting home from ten yards following a Steven Whittaker pass. On the hour mark, however, the visitors equalised from the penalty spot. With time running out late in the game, substitute Vladimir Weiss delivered a teasing cross from the left which defender Clancy hit past his own keeper to ensure a crucial 2-1 win for the defending champions.

APRIL

Although the Light Blues led twice against **Dundee United**, Peter Houston's side eventually secured all three points. Nikica Jelavic, from El-Hadji Diouf's perfectly placed free kick, guided a header past keeper Pernis for Rangers first but Robertson made it 1-1 right on the stroke of half time. In the second period, Steven Naismith's sizzling half volley restored the champions' advantage before Russell made it 2-2 with the second headed goal of the game. Right at the end, after Steven Whittaker hit the bar, Dundee United broke fast and Goodwillie slotted past Allan McGregor for the match winner.

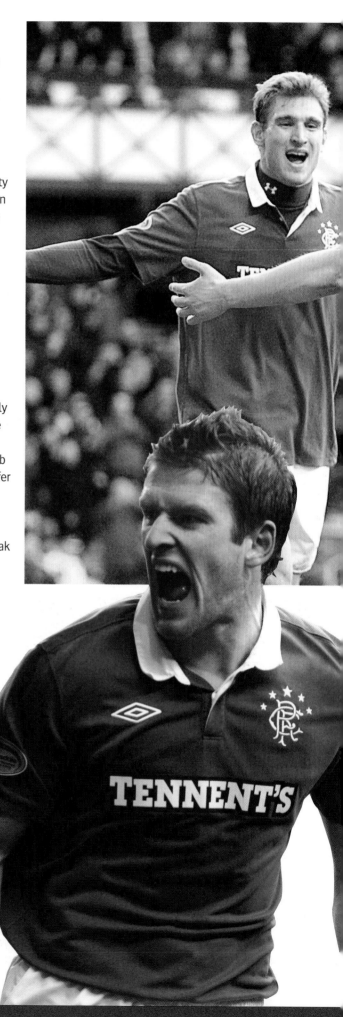

Kyle Lafferty pounced on a short headed back-pass by defender Grainger and coolly rounded the keeper for Rangers first goal against **St Johnstone** at McDiarmid Park. There were no additional first half goals although David Weir came close just before the break when he clipped the upright with a powerful header from a Gregg Wylde corner. Late in the second period after Allan McGregor had produced a couple of superb stops, Steven Naismith combined cleverly with Nikica Jelavic at the other end before dispatching a left foot drive into the bottom corner for a 2-0 win.

Hamilton Academical started confidently at New Douglas Park and indeed could have taken the lead after being awarded an early penalty. Allan McGregor pulled off a fine save however after diving to his right and blocking Imrie's spot kick. Then, as the first half drew to a close, Nikica Jelavic scored with a free kick from the edge of the area when he curled a delightful strike into the top corner of the net past Cerny in goal. Both keepers produced fine stops in the second period.

One goal also decided the outcome of Rangers next league game - **Aberdeen** at Pittodrie. Nikica Jelavic once again claimed the honour with his second exquisite finish in two games. This time the Croatian star had his back to goal as he controlled on his chest before executing the most perfect gymnastic overhead kick. In the blink of an eye, the ball flew past Langfield into the far corner for the striker's fourth goal in five games and his 11th in 13 SPL starts.

Rangers returned to the summit of the league table following a 2-1 win against **St Mirren**. In the first half, Sasa Papac netted from close range after Gallacher blocked Kyle Lafferty's shot but almost immediately central defender McGregor equalised for the visitors. A Steven Whittaker penalty conversion in the second period after Nikica Jelavic was fouled in the box made sure of the points.

An astonishing encounter at Tannadice ended with **Dundee United** reduced to 8 men after the home side had three players sent off for preventing separate goalscoring opportunities in the box. Steven Whittaker scored with two of the three subsequent penalties. Nikica Jelavic - a fine finish from a really tight angle after the keeper blocked a Steven Davis shot - and Kyle Lafferty (with a low drive from 25 yards) were the other scorers as Rangers cruised to a 4-0 win.

Although both sides created chances during the seventh and final Old Firm derby of the 2010/11 campaign, the game ended in deadlock at 0-0. Alan McGregor was once again in superlative form with three outstanding saves in the second half including a crucial penalty stop when he denied Samaras from 12 yards late in the game.

The penultimate away game for Walter Smith's side was against Scottish Cup finalists **Motherwell** - unbeaten in six games. Kyle Lafferty claimed the only goal of the first half when he charged into the box, rounded the keeper and netted from a tight angle despite the goal line efforts of defender Hammell. In the second half, Rangers played with style, pace and power, scoring another four. Steven Davis made it 2-0 when he steered home after a Steven Naismith drive had been blocked before Nikica Jelavic buried a powerful back post header from a perfect Sasa Papac cross. Finally Naismith, with two tremendous right foot strikes that both whistled past Randolph, took Rangers tally to five without reply.

MAY

Rangers welcomed new owner Craig Whyte to Ibrox with three first half goals against **Hearts**. Nikica Jelavic opened the scoring with a powerful left foot drive from a decreasing angle before Kyle Lafferty (with a low strike from a Gregg Wylde ball into the box) and Steven Davis – a headed finish from another Wylde delivery – netted just before the break. Although Steven Naismith and substitute David Healy both hit woodwork late-on, it was a Stevenson own goal that made it 4-0 on the night.

Against **Dundee United**, Nikica Jelavic again opened the scoring in the first period at Ibrox but this time the striker headed home following a Steven Whittaker cross. It was the Croatian's 18th goal in just 23 appearances for the Club. Four minutes later, Kyle Lafferty doubled the advantage with a clinical, first-touch finish when he stroked home following an inch perfect Steven Naismith pass. From a defensive point of view, Allan McGregor had now recorded eight clean sheets in the last nine league games. With just one more SPL fixture to play, Rangers knew that victory against Kilmarnock would confirm both the championship and three-in-a-row league titles for the Club.

Walter Smith's side started like a whirlwind at Rugby Park and virtually blew **Kilmarnock** away with three goals in the first seven minutes. Following a Steven Davis headed through ball almost immediately after kick-off, Kyle Lafferty lobbed the keeper for Rangers first of the game. Then Steven Naismith scored with a blistering left foot drive before Lafferty, after a perfect pass from Nikica Jelavic, guided home past the keeper for his second goal. After the break, Jelavic scored with a free-kick and Lafferty completed his hat-trick after slotting under the keeper. Kilmarnock's consolation goal from a deflected free-kick was immaterial as the SPL trophy was by this time already decked in red, white and blue ribbons. Walter Smith's second spell as manager had ended in the best possible way.

CHAMPIONS!

Player Profiles

Neil Alexander

BORN: Edinburgh, Scotland
DATE OF BIRTH: 10.03.1978
HEIGHT: 1.85m (6ft 1in)
POSITION: Goalkeeper
SENIOR CAREER: Stenhousemuir (1996-98), Livingston (1998-2001), Cardiff City (2001-07), Ipswich Town (2007-08)
SIGNED FOR RANGERS: January 2008
SEASON 2010/11 FIRST TEAM APPEARANCES (SUBSTITUTE): SPL 1 (0) Scottish Cup 0 (0) Co-operative Insurance Cup 4 (0) Europe 2 (0)

Allan McGregor

BORN: Edinburgh, Scotland
DATE OF BIRTH: 31.01.1982
HEIGHT: 1.83m (6ft)
POSITION: Goalkeeper
SENIOR CAREER: Rangers (2001 -), St Johnstone, (2004 loan), Dunfermline Athletic (2005 loan)
SIGNED FOR RANGERS: Product of Rangers Youth Team
SEASON 2010/11 FIRST TEAM APPEARANCES (SUBSTITUTE): SPL 37 (0) Scottish Cup 3 (0) Co-operative Insurance Cup 0 (0) Europe 8 (0)

Kirk Broadfoot

BORN: Irvine, Scotland
DATE OF BIRTH: 08.08.1984
HEIGHT: 1.91m (6ft 3ins)
POSITION: Defender
SENIOR CAREER: St Mirren (2002-07)
SIGNED FOR RANGERS: July 2007
SEASON 2010/11 FIRST TEAM APPEARANCES
(SUBSTITUTE): SPL 5 (3) Scottish Cup 0 (0) Co-operative
Insurance Cup 2 (0) Europe 4 (0)

Steven Whittaker

BORN: Edinburgh, Scotland
DATE OF BIRTH: 16.06.1984
HEIGHT: 1.85m (6ft 1in)
POSITION: Defender
SENIOR CAREER: Hibernian (2002-07)
SIGNED FOR RANGERS: August 2007
SEASON 2010/11 FIRST TEAM APPEARANCES
(SUBSTITUTE): SPL 36 (0) Scottish Cup 3 (0)
Co-operative Insurance Cup 3 (0) Europe 9 (0)
GOALS: 7

Sasa Papac

BORN: Mostar, Bosnia
DATE OF BIRTH: 07.02.1980
HEIGHT: 1.85m (6ft 1in)
Position: Defender
SENIOR CAREER: Karnten (2001-04),
Austria Vienna (2004-06)
SIGNED FOR RANGERS: August 2006
SEASON 2010/11 FIRST TEAM APPEARANCES
(SUBSTITUTE): SPL 34 (0) Scottish Cup 3 (0)
Co-operative Insurance Cup 2 (0) Europe 7 (0)
GOALS: 3

David Weir

BORN: Falkirk, Scotland
DATE OF BIRTH: 10.05.1970
HEIGHT: 1.91m (6ft 3ins)
POSITION: Defender
SENIOR CAREER: Falkirk (1992-96), Hearts (1996-99),
Everton (1999 – 2007)
SIGNED FOR RANGERS: January 2007
SEASON 2010/11 FIRST TEAM APPEARANCES
(SUBSTITUTE): SPL 37 (0) Scottish Cup 3 (0)
Co-operative Insurance Cup 3 (0) Europe 10 (0)

Maurice Edu

BORN: Fontana, California, USA
DATE OF BIRTH: 18.04.1986
HEIGHT: 1.83m (6ft)
POSITION: Midfielder
SENIOR CAREER: Toronto FC (2007-08)
SIGNED FOR RANGERS: August 2008
SEASON 2010/11 FIRST TEAM APPEARANCES
(SUBSTITUTE): SPL 27 (6) Scottish Cup 2 (0)
Co-operative Insurance Cup 3 (0) Europe 8 (0)
GOALS: 5

Lee McCulloch

BORN: Bellshill, Scotland
DATE OF BIRTH: 14.05.1978
HEIGHT: 1.85m (6ft 1in)
POSITION: Midfielder
SENIOR CAREER: Motherwell (1995-2001), Wigan
Athletic (2001-07)
SIGNED FOR RANGERS: July 2007
SEASON 2010/11 FIRST TEAM APPEARANCES
(SUBSTITUTE): SPL 17 (4) Scottish Cup 1 (1)
Co-operative Insurance Cup 2 (1) Europe 5 (0)
GOALS: 1

THE MANAGERS

After a three and a half year period as assistant to Walter Smith, Ally McCoist became Manager of Rangers prior to the 2011/12 campaign. He followed in the footsteps of:

William Wilton 1899-1920
8 League Championships and
1 Scottish Cup

Bill Struth 1920-1954
18 League Championships,
10 Scottish Cups and 2 League Cups

Scott Symon 1954-1967
6 League Championships,
5 Scottish Cups and 4 League Cups

Davie White 1967-1969

Willie Waddell 1969-1972
1 European Cup Winners' Cup
and 1 League Cup

Jock Wallace 1972- 1978
3 League Championships,
3 Scottish Cups and 2 League Cups

John Greig 1978-1983
2 Scottish Cups and 2 League Cups

Jock Wallace 1983 -1986
2 League Cups

Graeme Souness 1986-1991
3 League Championships
and 4 League Cups

Walter Smith 1991-1998
7 League Championships,
3 Scottish Cups and 3 League Cups

Dick Advocaat 1998-2001
2 League Championships,
2 Scottish Cups and 1 League Cup

Alex McLeish 2001-2006
2 League Championships,
2 Scottish Cups and 3 League Cups

Paul le Guen 2006 -2007

Walter Smith 2007-2011
3 League Championships,
2 Scottish Cups and 3 League Cups

Ally McCoist scored a record 355 goals for Rangers and was the Club's leading scorer in nine of his 15 seasons at Ibrox as a player. During that time he netted no fewer than 28 hat-tricks. He holds the Rangers record for league and European goals and was the first Scottish player to win Europe's prestigious Golden Boot trophy.

LORDS OF THE WING

ALAN MORTON After being appointed Manager of the Club in June 1920, Bill Struth's first signing was a small (five foot, four inch), slim (nine stone) winger from amateur side Queen's Park who would become one of the greatest of all Rangers players. Today, an oil portrait of Alan Morton takes pride of place above the splendid marble staircase inside the main entrance to Ibrox Stadium.

In addition to wonderful balance and ball control that enabled him to weave and drift past defenders with ease, Alan Morton was deadly with either foot. He played on the left wing despite being naturally right-footed and, for additional mobility, preferred only three studs on each boot as opposed to the normal four. Despite the exceptional heavy footballs of the time, superbly accurate crosses were routine and his trademark 'floating lob' into the penalty area was famous in the Scottish game.

Against Celtic, Morton was a revelation and, indeed, scored on his Old Firm league debut when Rangers

Rangers team group: (back row, l-r) Director Annean Graham, Director WG Small, Director John McPherson, Chairman Joseph Buchanan, James Bowie, Secretary WR Simpson (middle row, l-r) A Archibald, G Henderson, R Manderson, W Robb, T Gray, Andy Cunningham, A Dixon, Davie Meiklejohn (front row, l-r) Manager Bill Struth, W McCaudless, Thomas Muirhead, T Gavin, Alan Morton, J Jamieson, trainer Gt Riviestone defeated Celtic 2-1 in October 1920. Rangers won the league title that season with only one defeat along the way.

When Scotland crushed England 5-1 in 1928, the Wembley Wizards were born. Alan Morton was quite sensational that day with three of his inch-perfect crosses being the basis for an Alex Jackson hat-trick. Seemingly, it was during this game that an exasperated English fan called him a 'Wee Blue Devil' and the name stuck. In total, he wore the dark blue of Scotland 31 times.

1928 was, indeed, a special year for the player. Apart from the famous win against the 'Auld Enemy' he was a member of the emotionally triumphant Rangers team that defeated Celtic 4-0 at Hampden to lift the Scottish Cup for the first time in 25 years.

After announcing his retirement just after the start of Season 1932/33, Alan Morton became a director of the Club. Over a 13 year playing career at Rangers, he had won nine League Championships and two Scottish Cups, making 440 appearances and scoring 105 goals.

DAVIE COOPER One of the Light Blues most naturally gifted sons, Davie Cooper signed from Clydebank in June 1977 for £100,000 after starring against his boyhood heroes in three League Cup ties the previous campaign. Less than one year later, Rangers celebrated a domestic treble with the influential Cooper having started in all but two games throughout the season. He claimed his first Old Firm goal in the 2-1 League Cup final win of March 1978.

In the August 1979 Drybrough Cup final, Cooper scored one of the greatest goals ever seen at Hampden when he juggled past four totally bemused Celtic defenders before netting Rangers third goal in the 3-1 win. In truth, cup finals seemed to bring out the very best of him.

Few fans will ever forget his ferociously accurate free-kick that screamed past Aberdeen's Scotland keeper Jim Leighton in the League Cup final of 1987 or his stunning display against Dundee United in the 1981 Scottish Cup final replay when he tore the heart from a tangerine rearguard incapable of stopping him.

Such was his importance to the Club at this time, it was often said that if Cooper was on form, then so were Rangers. When the team managed by Graeme Souness became Scottish Champions in May 1987 – it was Rangers first league title since 1978 – Davie Cooper missed just two games in the entire campaign.

With appearances for Rangers declining over the next couple of years, the lure of regular first team football was hard to resist and Cooper joined Motherwell – managed by former team mate Tommy McLean - in 1989. Indeed, he enjoyed a new lease of life at Fir Park and produced many vintage performances for the Lanarkshire side. Then, in 1993, he returned to his first club Clydebank and the circle was complete.

Tragically - aged only 39 - Davie Cooper passed away on 23 March 1995 following a brain haemorrhage the day before.

First and foremost a Rangers man, Davie Cooper was once asked to describe the highlights of his time at Ibrox. He simply replied 'I played for the team I loved.'

The Co-operative Insurance Cup 2010/11

First action in defence of the Co-operative Insurance Cup was a home tie against First Division leaders **Dunfermline** when Nikica Jelavic and Kyle Lafferty were paired in attack. Both players certainly excelled and between them scored five times in an emphatic 7-2 win. Madjid Bougherra and Steven Naismith netted the other two goals on a night when Lafferty claimed his first hat-trick for the Club.

In the next round, a stunning half-volley from 18 yards by Northern Ireland striker Andrew Little opened the scoring at Rugby Park against **Kilmarnock**. This was the only goal of the first half. Then, after Pascali was denied by a superb Neil Alexander save at the start of the second period, former local hero Steven Naismith made doubly sure of Rangers progress into the last four of the 2010/11 competition when he fired home across the keeper following winger Gregg Wylde's low ball from the left.

Rangers then faced **Motherwell** (now managed by nine-in-a-row Club legend Stuart McCall) at Hampden at the semi-final stage of the competition. Maurice Edu scored the only goal of an even first half when the midfielder thumped home with a left foot strike from the edge of the box. Although Lasley equalised for Motherwell midway through the second period, Steven Naismith booked Rangers place in the final of the tournament ten minutes later when he headed past Randolph following a cross from the left by Nikica Jelavic. This was Naismith's 9th goal of the current campaign. Walter Smith, during his time as Manager and Assistant Manager in Glasgow, had now guided Rangers to 12 League Cup finals.

Against **Celtic** on cup final day, it was end-to-end play right from the start with both sides creating chances. Midway through the first period, half of Hampden erupted when Rangers scored. Steven Davis won possession and burst forward before steering home with a left foot shot from the edge of the box that rolled home off the

post. Seven minutes later, Celtic drew level after Ledley headed past Neil Alexander. Although there were no more goals before the interval, there was certainly some confusion shortly after Celtic's equaliser when referee Thomson awarded Rangers a penalty before promptly changing his mind. The second half was finely balanced with neither team managing to increase their one goal tally. However, seven minutes into extra-time, Jelavic - cleverly anticipating a quick free-kick by substitute Vladimir Weiss - claimed the winner when he outpaced central defender Mulgrew to send a low shot past Forster and in off the very same post that Davis clipped for the opening goal of the game.

Since the competition was first introduced back in Season 1946/47, Rangers had now won the League Cup tournament a record 27 times.

Summer Signings

Juan Manuel Ortiz

Spaniard Juan Manuel Ortiz was Ally McCoist's first new signing as manager of Rangers. The player, a graduate of Atletico Madrid's youth system, had loan spells with Osasuna (former Rangers player Carlos Cuellar was a team-mate here) and Poli Ejido (where he scored nine times in 40 games) before joining Almeria for the start of the 2007/08 La Liga campaign. The right-sided midfielder - who is equally at home on the left wing or in both full-back positions - played 126 games in four years for Almeria prior to arriving at Rangers after agreeing a three-year deal.

Lee Wallace

Lee Wallace joined Rangers on a five-year contract after seven seasons and 140 appearances with Hearts. His first goal for the Edinburgh club was in February 2005 when he scored the opener in a 3-1 win against Kilmarnock in the Scottish Cup at Rugby Park. Last season, the full back was appointed team vice captain at Tynecastle by manager Jim Jefferies. Earlier in his career, Wallace - starting every game at left back - was an integral part of the Scotland Under-19 team that went all the way to the final of the 2006 UEFA Under-19 Championships before losing to Spain.

Matt McKay

Matt McKay was a key member of the Brisbane Roar side that dominated the 2010/11 Hyundai A-League season in Australia. The midfielder was subsequently named captain of the Players' Team of the Season at the end of that victorious campaign. McKay also enjoyed a superb AFC Asian Cup with Australia in January 2011. In addition to setting up former Liverpool star Harry Kewell for the quarter-final winner against Iraq, he was named Man of the Match following an impressive display in the semi-final demolition of Uzbekistan when he set up three of his side's six goals.

Kyle Bartley returned to the Club on-loan from Arsenal for a second season. The young central defender started a total of nine league and cup games last season and scored the only goal of the game at New St Mirren Park in early March 2011. However, an unfortunate knee injury sustained later that month at Ibrox during the Europa League Cup tie against PSV Eindhoven prematurely ended his 2010/11 campaign.

Of Colombian descent, United States central midfielder Alejandro Bedoya was born in New Jersey and played college soccer for Boston University and Farleigh Dickinson University before joining Swedish club Orebro in January 2009. He won his first international start with the senior United States national team in a friendly against Brazil in August 2010 and made five appearances in the Gold Cup tournament in the summer of 2011 when the USA reached the final before losing to Mexico.

Carlos Bocanegra

Carlos Bocanegra made over 100 appearances in the Premiership with Fulham during his time at Craven Cottage from 2004 to 2008. In Season 2006/07, the defender was the London club's second leading scorer with five goals. Bocanegra then moved to France and spent two seasons with Rennes before joining fellow Ligue 1 side Saint Etienne for the start of Season 2010/11. Captain of the USA since 2007, he has made over 90 appearances for his country including the memorable 2-0 semi-final win over Spain during the 2009 FIFA Confederations Cup.

Dorin Goian

Towering central defender Dorin Goian rose to prominence during his four seasons with Steaua Bucharest in Romania from 2005 to 2009. During that time in his homeland, he was linked with a possible move to Manchester United. The player headed for Italy to join Serie A side Palermo at the Renzo Barbero stadium in Sicily for the start of the 2009/10 campaign. When the Sicilians stunned league leaders AC Milan in March 2011, it was Goian who famously scored the only goal of the game. The defender is an extremely experienced international, having played over 35 times for his country. He scored the winner for Romania against Holland in 2007.

THE EUROPEAN CAMPAIGNS SEASON 2010/11

UEFA Champions League

As well as Rangers, Group C of the 2010/11 UEFA Champions League tournament comprised **Manchester United**, **Valencia** (Spain) and **Bursaspor** of Turkey.

Away to **Manchester United** in the first game, Walter Smith's game plan of a 5-4-1 defensive formation worked to perfection and a superbly disciplined Rangers unit emerged from Old Trafford with a valuable point following the 0-0 draw. It was an epic rearguard display of true grit and determination by the Ibrox men.

Turkish champions **Bursapor** arrived at Ibrox with a 100% record in their domestic league. Steven Naismith scored the only goal of the game in the first half when he netted from close range following Kirk Broadfoot's cushioned header into the box from a superb Steven Whittaker cross-field ball. This was Rangers first win in 13 European matches.

Despite a sparkling display against Spanish giants **Valencia**, Rangers had to finally settle for a 1-1 draw. Ibrox was really rocking after half an hour when Maurice Edu, from a Vladimir Weiss corner, jumped highest in the penalty area to head purposefully past Cesar in goal. Unfortunately, right at the start of the second half from a teasing Valencia corner into a crowded penalty area, the American international then headed past Allan McGregor to square the game. Having created the better chances throughout the ninety minutes, Walter Smith's side probably deserved more than just a share of the spoils.

Valencia proved too strong for the SPL champions on match day four of the tournament. Although Steven

Naismith smashed off the post with a powerful right foot drive early-on in the Mestalla Stadium, the home side gradually took control and eventually won 3-0 courtesy of one goal in the first half and two in the second.

A late Wayne Rooney penalty conversion was all that separated Rangers and visitors **Manchester United** in the next game. Despite this 1-0 defeat, Rangers still finished third in the group and gained automatic entry into the last 32 of the Europa League competition.

Kenny Miller opened the scoring early-on against **Bursaspor** in the Ataturk Stadium with a terrific curling left foot shot from 15 yards following a Steven Whittaker cross. The Turks equalised late in the game however to deny Rangers their second group win of the 2010/11 tournament.

Europa League

Steven Whittaker powered home with a header in the second period at Ibrox to give Rangers the lead against **Sporting Lisbon**. However, a Fernandez goal towards the end of the ninety minutes meant that the Light Blues needed to win or achieve a higher-scoring draw than 1-1 in the return leg in Portugal to progress further in the competition.

At the Estadio Jose Alvalade in Lisbon, El-Hadji Diouf scored his first goal for the Club when he headed past Patricio from a floating Steven Davis cross. Former Ibrox favourite Pedro Mendes then equalised for **Sporting Lisbon** just before the break. In the second half, all seemed lost for Rangers when Djalo headed past Allan McGregor but just before the final whistle Maurice Edu made it 2-2 from very close range after Richard Foster made space on the right before delivering a perfect ball into the box.

Next up was **PSV Eindhoven** of Holland. Although Rangers emerged unscathed from the Philips Stadion following a battling 0-0 draw in the first leg in Holland, a 1-0 reversal at Ibrox one week later meant that the Dutch outfit progressed to the quarter-final stage of the tournament as another European journey came to an end.

THE EUROPEAN CUP WINNERS' CUP 1972

2012 is the 40th Anniversary of Rangers most famous European victory

The Road to the Final

First round
1st Leg	Rennes 1	Rangers 1
		Johnston (68)
2nd Leg	Rangers 1	Rennes 0

Second Round
1st Leg	Rangers 3	Sporting Lisbon 2
	Stein (9, 19)	
	Henderson (28)	
2nd Leg	Sporting Lisbon 4	Rangers 3
		Stein (27, 46)
		Henderson (100)
		After extra time

Quarter Final
1st Leg	Torino 1	Rangers 1
		Johnston (12)
2nd Leg	Rangers 1	Torino (0)
	MacDonald (46)	

Semi Final
1st Leg	Bayern Munich 1	Rangers 1
		Zobel og (49)
2nd Leg	Rangers 2	Bayern Munich 0
	Jardine (1)	
	Parlane (23)	

Final – 24 May 1972, Nou Camp Stadium, Barcelona

Rangers 3	Moscow Dynamo 2
Stein (24)	
Johnston (40, 49)	

Rangers: McCloy, Jardine, Mathieson, Greig, Johnstone, Smith, McLean, Conn, Stein, MacDonald, Johnston.

Player Profiles

Steven Davis

BORN: Ballymena, Northern Ireland
DATE OF BIRTH: 01.01.1985
HEIGHT: 1.73m (5ft 8ins)
POSITION: Midfielder
SENIOR CAREER: Aston Villa (2003-07), Fulham (2007-08), Rangers (2008 loan)
SIGNED FOR RANGERS: August 2008
SEASON 2010/11 FIRST TEAM APPEARANCES (SUBSTITUTE): SPL 37 (0) Scottish Cup 3 (0) Co-operative Insurance Cup 3 (0) Europe 10 (0)
GOALS: 5

Jamie Ness

BORN: Troon, Scotland
DATE OF BIRTH: 02.03.1991
HEIGHT: 1.87m (6ft 1in)
POSITION: Midfielder
SENIOR CAREER: (2010 -)
SIGNED FOR RANGERS: Product of Rangers Youth Policy
SEASON 2010/11 FIRST TEAM APPEARANCES (SUBSTITUTE): SPL 8 (3) Scottish Cup 2 (0) Co-operative Insurance Cup 0 (0) Europe 0 (0)
GOALS: 1

Kyle Hutton

Gregg Wylde

Steven Naismith

Nikica Jelavic

Kyle Lafferty

BORN: Enniskillen, Northern Ireland
DATE OF BIRTH: 16.09.1987
HEIGHT: 1.93m (6ft 4ins)
POSITION: Striker
SENIOR CAREER: Burnley (2005 – 08),
Darlington (2006 loan)
SIGNED FOR RANGERS: June 2008
**SEASON 2010/11 FIRST TEAM APPEARANCES
(SUBSTITUTE)**: SPL 23 (8) Scottish Cup 1 (1)
Co-operative Insurance Cup 3 (0) Europe 3 (5)
GOALS: 15

John Fleck

BORN: Glasgow, Scotland
DATE OF BIRTH: 24.08.1991
HEIGHT: 1.69m (5ft 7ins)
POSITION: Striker
SENIOR CAREER: (2007 -)
SIGNED FOR RANGERS:
Product of Rangers Youth Policy
**SEASON 2010/11 FIRST TEAM APPEARANCES
(SUBSTITUTE)**: SPL 3 (10) Scottish Cup 1 (0)
Co-operative Insurance Cup 0 (1) Europe 1 (1)

TEN MEMORABLE GOALS FROM SEASON 2010/11

1

1. STEVEN NAISMITH
Home v Kilmarnock, August 2010

Steven Naismith's winning goal against Kilmarnock ensured a perfect start for Rangers on the opening day of the SPL campaign.

2. NIKICA JELAVIC
Away v Aberdeen, September 2010

Nikica Jelavic slotted home the winner as Rangers recorded their first victory against Aberdeen at Pittodrie since December 2006.

3. STEVEN NAISMITH
Away v Hearts, October 2010

Right at the end of the game, Steven Naismith ended a lung-bursting run from deep with a glorious strike for Rangers second - and winning - goal.

4. STEVEN NAISMITH
Home v Bursapor, September 2010

Steven Naismith scored the only goal of the game against Bursapor in the UEFA Champions League competition to record Rangers first win in 13 European outings.

5. KENNY MILLER
Away v Celtic, October 2010

Kenny Miller's deadly right foot volley established a 2-1 lead for the defending champions at Celtic Park in the first Old Firm encounter of the league campaign.

2

4

5

7

6. KYLE LAFFERTY

Home v Hearts, February 2011

The only goal of the game against high-flying Hearts was a perfect volley from fifteen yards scored by Kyle Lafferty shortly after kick-off.

7. STEVEN DAVIS

Hampden v Celtic, March 2011

In the final of the Co-operative Insurance Cup, Steven Davis opened the scoring against Celtic with a left foot shot that rolled home off the post.

8. NIKICA JELAVIC

Hampden v Celtic, March 2011

Nikica Jelavic netted the winner in extra-time when Rangers defeated Celtic at Hampden for the Club's record 27th League Cup.

9. NIKICA JELAVIC

Away v Hamilton Academical, April 2011

A superbly struck free kick from the edge of the area by Nikica Jelavic was all that separated the teams at New Douglas Park as the season headed to an exciting conclusion.

10. KYLE LAFFERTY

Away v Kilmarnock, May 2011

The crucial opening goal at Rugby Park on championship day was a perfectly judged lob over the Kilmarnock keeper by Kyle Lafferty.

10

STEVEN NAISMITH

Rangers Annual Player of the Year 2010/11

Steven Naismith began his senior career at Kilmarnock where he was named Scottish Football Writers' Player of the Year for Season 2005/06. At the end of the following 2006/07 campaign, he collected another Young Player of the Year award but this time it was from his fellow professionals. Naismith arrived at Ibrox on the August 2007 transfer deadline day and made his Rangers debut less than 24 hours later when he appeared, to great acclaim, as a substitute late-on in the SPL home game against Gretna.

His first goal for the Club was in the 3-0 win over Aberdeen in September 2007 but luck deserted him later that season when he was seriously injured during the Scottish Cup semi-final win against St Johnstone at Hampden. Coincidentally, it was against the same team in the same competition that the Scot returned to first team action in January 2009.

Naismith scored his side's winning goal in the 2-1 win against Kilmarnock at Ibrox on day one of the 2010/11 league season. In late September, Rangers recorded their first Pittodrie victory against Aberdeen since December 2006. Although Nikica Jelavic netted the decider that day, it was Naismith who created the goal after beating the offside trap and running from the halfway mark before drawing the keeper and supplying the decisive pass to the Croatian international. The following midweek, he scored the only goal of the game in the UEFA Champions League clash against Bursapor of Turkey for Rangers first win in 13 European games. Naismith then completed an excellent week for both himself and the Club when, three days later, he netted the late winner against Hearts at Tynecastle in the title race.

On the road to the final of the Co-operative Insurance Cup, he scored in every round of the competition against Dunfermline, Kilmarnock and Motherwell respectively. Indeed, his headed goal at the semi-final stage was the decider in the 2-1 win over Motherwell. Although Naismith was not on the score sheet against opponents Celtic on cup final day in late March, he once again thrilled the legions of Rangers fans at Hampden with his clever play and combative spirit.

The player was well to the fore as both scorer and creator of chances as the 2010/11 league campaign headed towards its dramatic conclusion. For example, he netted twice against Motherwell in Rangers penultimate away game, provided the inch perfect pass when Kyle Lafferty claimed number two against Dundee United in the last home fixture and scored his side's second goal on championship day at Rugby Park after starting and finishing the attack.

Steven Naismith – Rangers Annual Player of the Year for Season 2010/11.

Where is Whittaker aiming? Can you work out which one is the real ball? Answers p6?

SPOT THE DIFFERENCE

Can you see the five differences? Answers p61

HLADLINE NEWS

Rangers made the following football headlines last season. What was the occasion? Answers p61

Walter's final postscript

Stevie wonder

FEAST OF STEVEN

1.	IT'S NOT GRIM UP NORTH NOW	Daily Mail, 27.9.10
2.	STEVIE WONDER	Mail On Sunday, 3.10.10
3.	NO STOPPING CITY SLICKER	Mail On Sunday, 16.1.11
4.	BLUE SKIES CLEAR THE CLOUDS	Daily Mail, 28.2.11
5.	WELCOME TO JEL	Sun, 21.3.11
6.	WALTER'S FINAL POSTSCRIPT	Daily Mail, 21.3.11
7.	HIT FOR SIX	Sun, 6.4.11
8.	NIKICA MAGIC KEEPS RANGERS ALIVE AND BICYCLE KICKING	Daily Mail 14.4.11
9.	FEAST OF STEVEN	Sun, 18.4.11
10.	3MENDOUS	Sun, 16.5.11

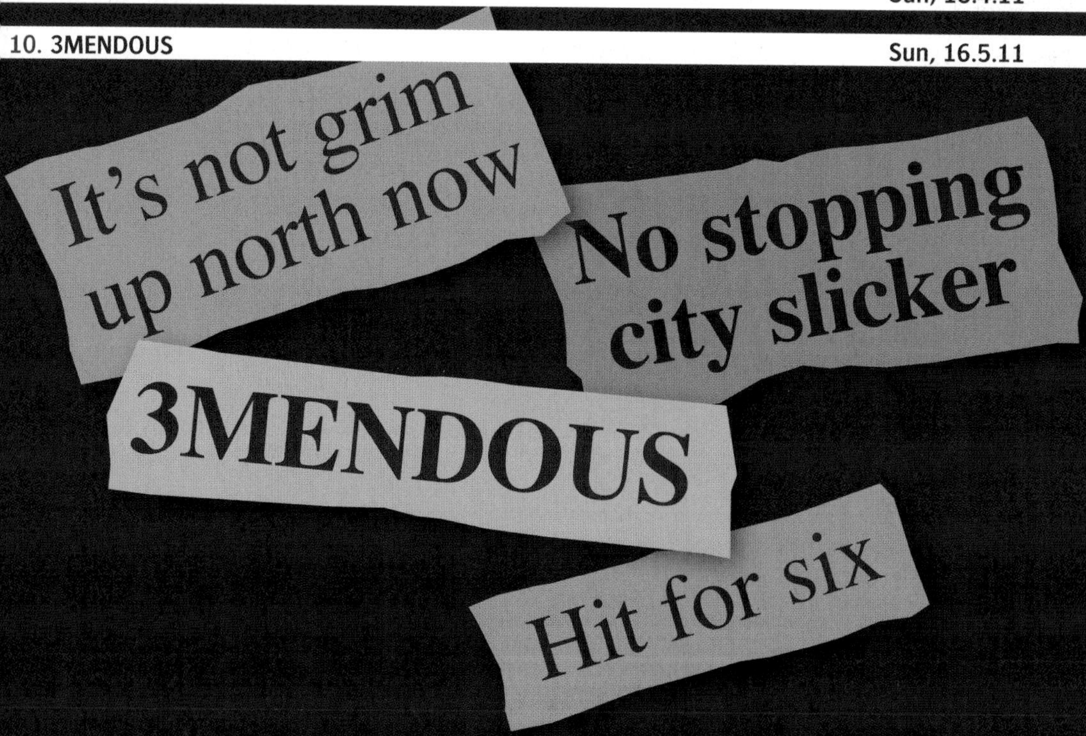

It's not grim up north now

No stopping city slicker

3MENDOUS

Hit for six

WHERE DID WE COME FROM?

Can you link these current players with the clubs from which they joined Rangers? Answers p61

1.	Steven Naismith	A Fulham
2.	Kyle Lafferty	B Ipswich Town
3.	Steven Whittaker	C Austria Vienna
4.	Steven Davis	D Rapid Vienna
5.	Lee McCulloch	E Hibernian
6.	Nikica Jelavic	F Toronto FC
7.	Sasa Papac	G Burnley
8.	Neil Alexander	H Kilmarnock
9.	Maurice Edu	I Wigan Athletic
10.	Kirk Broadfoot	J St Mirren

Junior Gers is the fantastic new membership scheme for Rangers fans aged 16 and under. Packed with a range of benefits including a membership pack, the chance to be selected as a matchday mascot and much more, this is the ultimate club for young football fans who want to get closer to Rangers.

Members are also in with a chance of being selected to attend player events and receive a 10% discount in the JJB Rangers Megastore and JJB stores on Rangers products*, a membership card, e-newsletter 4 times a year, e-birthday card (provided your birthday falls within the period of membership), e-certificate, e-Christmas card, discounted tickets to selected SPL matches** and more!

Junior Gers full season membership is priced at £12 for UK residents and £20 for overseas residents, juvenile season ticket holders automatically become members upon providing an email address and

can purchase a membership pack for the discounted price of £7.

Full season membership packs come in a Junior Gers gift box and include a Season 2011/12 scarf, Rangers pen and mini football keyring. Junior Gers full season membership sales close on 30 September 2011 and re-open for half season membership in November 2011.

Junior Gers half season membership packs come in a Junior Gers gift box containing a Season 2011/12 scarf and exclusive Rangers poster and are priced at £8.

Membership is valid until 31 May 2012 so the quicker
you sign up the longer you get the benefits for!

Junior Gers: 0871 702 1972^
Email: juniorgers@rangers.co.uk
Visit: www.rangers.co.uk/juniorgers

DREAM TEAM

If you were manager of Rangers and could sign any footballer in the world, who would you choose to play for Rangers? Fill in your dream team!

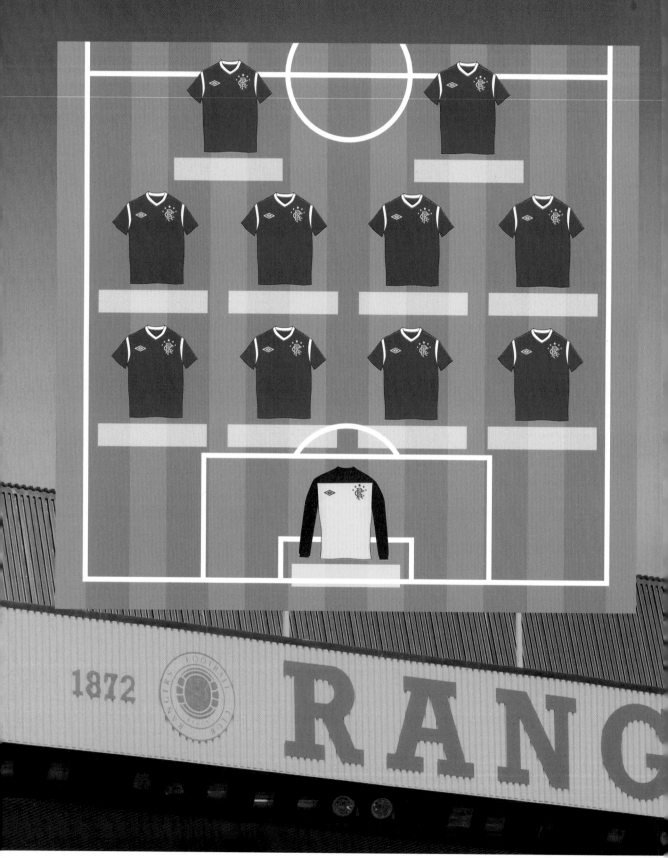

QUIZ ANSWERS

SPOT THE BALL (Page 54)

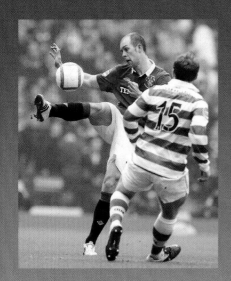

SPOT THE DIFFERENCE (Page 55)

HEADLINE NEWS (Page 56)

1. Rangers 3-2 away win against Aberdeen confirms a first Pittodrie league win since December 2006.
2. Steven Naismith nets a dramatic late winner against Hearts at Tynecastle three days after scoring the only goal of the game against Bursaspor in the UEFA Champions League.
3. On loan Manchester City winger Vladimir Weiss scores twice against Hamilton Academical in addition to winning a penalty for Rangers in the 4-0 win.
4. After losing to Celtic in the SPL, Rangers roar back with a 4-0 win against St Johnstone.
5. Nikica Jelavic scores the extra-time winner against Celtic in the final of the Co-operative Insurance Cup.
6. Walter Smith's last appearance at Hampden as manager of Rangers ends with triumph in the Co-operative Insurance Cup final.
7. After a 6pm kick-off, Rangers win away at St Johnstone.
8. A stunning overhead kick by Nikica Jelavic is the only goal of the game against Aberdeen at Pittodrie.
9. Steven Davis turns in a man-of-the-match display against St Mirren and Steven Whittaker scores the winning goal.
10. Rangers celebrate three-in-a-row following the championship success at Rugby Park.

WHERE DID WE COME FROM? (Page 57)

1-H	3-E	5-I	7-C	9-F
2-G	4-A	6-D	8-B	10-J